Protect Our Planet

Disappearing Wildlife

Angela Royston

Heinemann
LIBRARY

www.heinemann.co.uk/library
Visit our website to find out more information about Heinemann Library books.

To order:
☎ Phone 44 (0) 1865 888066
🖹 Send a fax to 44 (0) 1865 314091
💻 Visit the Heinemann Bookshop at www.heinemann.co.uk/library to browse our catalogue and order online.

First published in Great Britain by Heinemann Library, Halley Court, Jordan Hill, Oxford OX2 8EJ, part of Harcourt Education. Heinemann is a registered trademark of Harcourt Education Ltd.

© Harcourt Education Ltd 2008

Editorial: Sian Smith and Cassie Mayer
Design: Joanna Hinton-Malivoire
Picture research: Melissa Allison, Fiona Orbell and Erica Martin
Production: Duncan Gilbert
Printed and bound in China by South China Printing Co. Ltd.

ISBN 978 0 431 08478 7
12 11 10 09 08
10 9 8 7 6 5 4 3 2 1

British Library Cataloguing in Publication Data
Royston, Angela
    Disappearing wildlife. - (Protect our planet)
    1. Endangered species - Juvenile literature
    2. Wildlife conservation - Juvenile literature
    I. Title
    333.9'542

Acknowledgements
The publishers would like to thank the following for permission to reproduce photographs:
© Creatas p.**8**; © Digital Vision pp.**11**, **7**; © Ecoscene p.**15** (Fritz Polking); © Getty Images pp.**5** (Digital Vision), **17** (Minden Pictures), **12** (Photodisc); © NaturePL p.**20** (Martha Holmes); © Panos pp.**10** (Chris Stowers), **27** (Dominic Harcourt-Webster); © Pearson Education Ltd p.**29** (Tudor Photography. Leaflet covers courtesy of WWF-UK and Friends of the Earth.); © Photolibrary pp.**14** (Belinda Wright), **4**, **16** (Daniel Cox), **25** (Dave Fleetham), **26** (David Courtenay), **24** (Gerald Soury), **13** (L Husebye Terry), **21** (Mark Webster), **19** (Rob Nunnington), **23** (Wiesniewski Wiesniewski); © Still Pictures p.**6** (Fred Bruemmer); © WWF-Canon p.**28** (Michel Terrettaz).

Cover photograph of a polar bear reproduced with permission of © Getty Images (Sue Flood).

Every effort has been made to contact copyright holders of any material reproduced in this book. Any omissions will be rectified in subsequent printings if notice is given to the publishers.

Contents

Any words appearing in the text in bold, **like this**, are explained in the Glossary.

What is wildlife?

Wildlife is all the animals that live in the wild. It includes sea animals and land animals. It does not include cows, dogs, and other animals that are kept by people.

Butterflies and other insects are types of wildlife.

There are many different types of animals. Each type is called a **species**.

A leopard is a species of wild cat.

Endangered Species

Many types of animals that lived millions of years ago no longer exist. They are **extinct**. Dinosaurs are one type of animal that lived long ago. There are no dinosaurs alive today.

Mammoths are a type of elephant that no longer exists.

Today there are few mountain gorillas left in the wild.

Many **species** of animals are now in danger of becoming extinct. Gorillas are an **endangered** species. This means that there are so few wild gorillas they could die out altogether.

What is a habitat?

A **habitat** is the place where an animal lives. Many animals can only live in a certain habitat. For example, polar bears live in the very cold lands in the **Arctic**. Camels live in hot, dry **deserts**.

Polar bears have thick fur and layers of fat to keep them warm.

You can see different types of habitat on this map of the world. The oceans are habitats too!

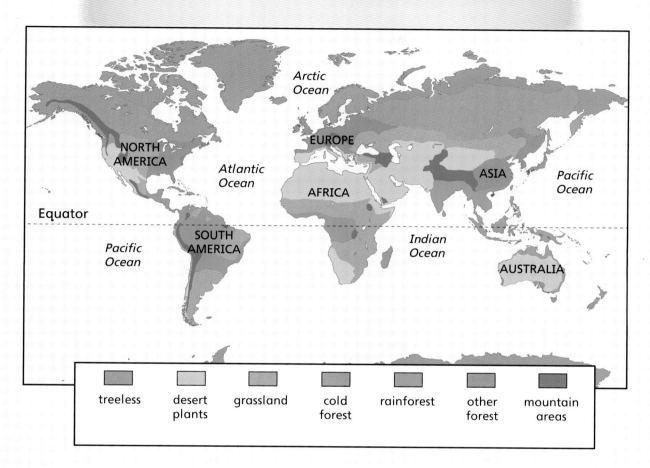

The world is divided into several main habitats. Each main habitat includes many smaller habitats. Even your local park is a habitat!

Changing habitats

Habitats sometimes change. If a habitat changes very quickly, most of the animals that live there die. Habitats change for many different reasons. Sometimes people damage or destroy habitats.

This wasteland is a habitat. The habitat will be destroyed when new offices are built.

Land at an airport is covered by concrete.
Most wildlife cannot live here.

Building towns, airports, and roads destroys
many natural habitats. The animals that live
there die or move somewhere else. The new
habitats have very little **wildlife**.

Farming

This large field is used to grow only one type of crop.

Farmers change natural **habitats**. Most natural habitats have a mixture of plants and many **species** of **wildlife**. Farmers plant just one type of **crop** in their fields. This means that fewer animals can live on that land.

Most farmers spray their crops to kill **pests** that harm the crop. The spray also kills butterflies, bees, and other wildlife that do not harm the crops. Very few animals live in these fields.

Planes are used to spray large areas of crops.

Disappearing habitats

Some animals need lots of space to survive. For example, tigers have to hunt over a wide area to find enough food. As more land is used for farms and cities, tigers are in danger of becoming **extinct**.

Three **species** of tiger have recently become extinct.

Pandas need to spend at least 12 hours a day eating bamboo.

Pandas live in China and eat only bamboo shoots. Much of the land where bamboo used to grow has been cleared to make farmland. Pandas are now **endangered** because they cannot find enough bamboo to eat.

Cutting down forests

Rainforests are forests that grow in warm, wet places in the world. People are clearing large areas of rainforest. They cut down the trees to make farmland.

Orang-utans in Indonesia are **endangered**. The rainforest where they live is being destroyed.

These frogs come from the rainforest.

Millions of different **species** live in rainforests. Many of these species are not found anywhere else. Scientists are afraid that some of these species will become **extinct**.

Changing climates

The Earth is getting warmer. This is called **global warming**. Global warming is changing the **climate** in many places. This means that the weather those places usually get is changing. As the climate changes, the **habitats** change too.

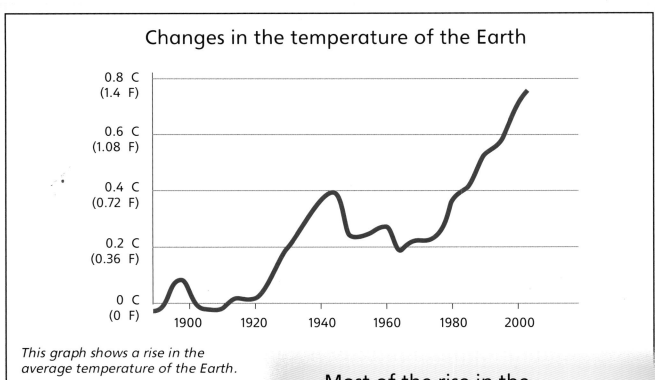

Changes in the temperature of the Earth

This graph shows a rise in the average temperature of the Earth.

Most of the rise in the temperature of the Earth has happened in the last few years.

Only a few **species** can live in a desert.

Many places get more rain than they used to, but many others get less rain. Less rain makes the ground dry up and the plants die. When **grasslands** dry up they become **deserts**. Giraffes and other animals that live on the grassland have to leave.

Warmer waters

The sea is warming up. This is making the ice in the **Arctic** melt. Polar bears creep across the ice to hunt for seals in the sea. When the ice melts, they cannot reach the seals. If too much ice melts, polar bears may become **extinct**.

Some scientists think the polar bear could become extinct in 100 years.

coral

When a coral reef dies, the fish and other animals that live around it disappear.

Warmer seas are damaging **coral reefs**. Coral reefs are like ridges of rock. They are made of millions of tiny **shellfish**. If the sea becomes too warm for them, the tiny shellfish die.

Hunting and poaching

Some animals are hunted by people. Elephants are hunted for their long ivory **tusks**. The tusks are carved into ornaments and jewellery.

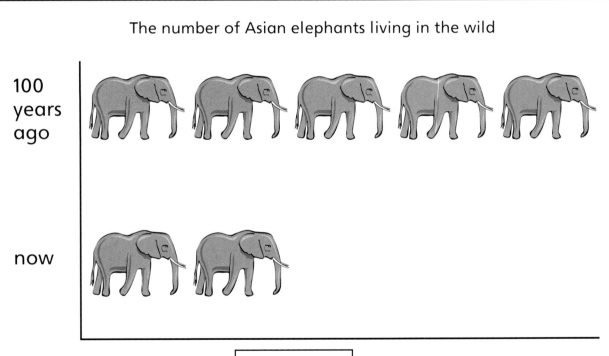

The number of Asian elephants living in the wild

100 years ago

now

= 20,000

Poachers sell the horns of black rhinos for a lot of money.

Poachers are people who hunt animals illegally. Some poachers kill **endangered species**, such as black rhinos in Africa. The black rhinos are killed because their horns are used in some medicines.

Endangered sea animals

Some animals that live in the sea are also **endangered**. Some **species** of whales are endangered because they were hunted in the past. Many were hunted for their meat.

This is a gray whale. Hunting nearly caused these whales to become **extinct**.

dolphin

Some sea animals are killed by accident. In parts of the Pacific Ocean, dolphins and tuna often swim together. These dolphins can be killed by accident when they are caught in fishing nets with the tuna.

Protecting wildlife

One way to protect **wildlife** is to make national parks. A national park is a large area of land where the **habitats** are protected. The wildlife is protected, too.

National parks are made where animals normally live. The land this elephant lives on has been made into a national park.

People who work for the national parks try to stop **poachers** from killing the animals. Some people say that parts of the ocean should also be made into national parks.

Charities that protect wildlife

Many **charities** work to protect **wildlife** and its **habitats**. They tell people about **endangered species** and the threats to the environment. They raise money to protect animals and the places they live.

This baby orang-utan has no parents to teach it how to survive in the wild. It is being helped by a charity in Malaysia.

You can become a member of charities that help protect wildlife.

You can help protect wildlife, too. Ask your librarian to help you learn more about wildlife in your area. Look up local charities that help protect wildlife. Everyone needs to work together to protect our wildlife.

Glossary

Arctic land and ocean around the North Pole where it is very cold all year round

charity group of people who collect money and spend it on helping to make things better

climate kind of weather a place usually gets

coral reef ridge of hard coral made of the shells of billions of tiny shellfish

crop plants grown by farmers to sell or use

desert area of dry land that gets very little rain

endangered in danger of becoming extinct

extinct when no members of a species exist any longer

global warming rise in temperature of the surface of the Earth, including the land, sea, and air

grassland land where the main plants are grasses. Grasslands are called prairies in North America and savannahs in Africa.

habitat place where particular kinds of plants grow and particular kinds of animals live

pest animal that eats farm crops

poacher person who hunts animals illegally

shellfish kind of animal that lives in the water and has a hard shell around its body

species group of very similar plants or animals that can produce new plants or animals of the same type

tusk extra-long tooth that grows outside the mouth

vet doctor that heals animals

wildlife animals that live without interference from people

Find out more

Books to read

Save our Animals! Save the Giant Panda, Louise and Richard Spilsbury (Heinemann Library, 2006)

The Best Book of Endangered and Extinct Animals, Christiane Gunzi, (Kingfisher, 2004)

Websites to visit

www.wwf.org.uk/gowild/index.asp
This website was set up by the World Wildlife Fund. It includes information about habitats and games to play.

www.fws.gov/endangered/kids/index.html
This website has information about endangered animals and includes links to many other sites.

www.kidinfo.com/science/endangered–animals.html
This website gives information about endangered animals.

Index